ENDLESS

A LITERATE PASSION

SAINT JULIAN PRESS

POETRY SERIES

"*ENDLESS* is a mantic book, the handiwork of a sorceress and *magicienne*, of one whose gifts with language and perception transform the sublunary and timely into pictures of dynamic affect. This poetry transforms the reader as it moves through the emotion and times of character, literature, and place; there is much profound learning in this book and its magisterial scales of language. It is refreshing and rare to read such flawless poetry…To put the collection aside is suddenly to see a landscape in a new light where grey and white are perpetually moving but without invention or causality: for such is the mastery of the author that each phrase and metaphor, each image and stanza, resonates perfectly. Hence, ENDLESS is made into an object I return to frequently and continue to keep with me.'"

~Kevin McGrath, *Harvard University*

"Moving page by page through the red silk journals of the heart, Anne Tammel takes the reader on a journey through a historical and literary landscape so vibrant, so vividly and generously splashed with color and love that it could only be explored through poetry. Here is a woman, who, much like the great artists about whom she writes, not only looks at the world with extraordinary, resplendent vision, but who has the courage and talent to offer that vision beautifully to the world."

~Melissa Studdard, *I Ate the Cosmos for Breakfast*

"*ENDLESS* reads like a love letter, not only to the iconic authors and adventurers of the 20th century whose personas she authentically inhabits, but as an epistle to her own love of life…I feel as if I'm inside a museum of daring sculptures, a Grecian sun glinting off the bone white marble. The collection – voluptuous. Its rhythms searching, sensual, and authentic *like a wife–an insatiable wife…a lover of silk…and words…and your breath*, finding the authentic voice within the poet's internal theater. I slipped easily into these literary shoes to stride confidently across the stage. Whether she walks with the beatniks or Mephistopheles, Tammel enters Borge's questioning labyrinth, and we leave her archetypal maze deeply touched…changed."

~Lois P. Jones, *Kyoto Poetry Journal*

Also by

Anne Tammel

Paper Angels

Endless

A Literate Passion

Poems

by

Anne Tammel

Saint Julian Press
Houston

Published by Saint Julian Press, Inc.
2053 Cortlandt, Suite 200
Houston, Texas 77008
www.saintjulianpress.com

Copyright © 2015, Anne Tammel
All rights reserved.

ISBN-13: 978-0-9965231-0-3
ISBN-10: 0996523103
Library of Congress Control Number: 2015957592

Cover Art: *Anais and Henry,* by Eric Anfinson, inspired by the author, Anne Tammel, as well as Anais Nin and Henry Miller, two characters who appear in *Endless: A Literate Passion.* Permission granted graciously by the artist. www.ericanfinson.com

Cover Design: Anne Tammel

*To my sweetheart and my muse and my
literate passion for all time,
Mr. Tammel.*

TABLE OF CONTENTS

PASSIONE: *That Red Red Sea* — 1
  Amelia Earhart at the Red Sea — 3
  Paper Angels — 8
  Amelia and the Silken Sheet — 10
  Blue Angels — 12
  Poland and the Thick Black Shoes — 14
  Imaginary Birds — 16

MAGIA: *Fire, Sage and Mist* — 21
  She Dreamt — 23
  Fire, Spice and Zen — 24
  Ominous Structures — 25
  Candlelight: *The Lonely Pond* — 27
  Selene: *Moonrise Over Oia* — 28

VITA DELL'ALDILÀ: *Euphoric Wings* — 31
  Proliferative Ashes: *For Paul Celan* — 33
  Streets of August — 35
  Double Sunrise: *Anne Morrow to Charles Lindbergh* — 36
  Tohoku — 37

PERDITA: *In the Silent Light* — 41
  Kerouac in San Francisco — 43
  Unripe Peaches — 45
  Marilyn — 47

SPIRITO: *Mystical Minoan Chimes*	53
Dante and the Silk Journal	55
Gates of Paradise: *Polythene Wings*	56
Athênai	57
Leaving Paris: *Zelda to F. Scott Fitzgerald*	58
AURORA BOREALE: *Milkweed Honey, Pure Saffron Desire*	61
Paradiso: *Eros & Psyche*	63
Endless: *Anaïs Nin to Henry Miller*	64
Dinner Couplets	65
Autumn, Love, and Pomegranate Pears	67
Moon an Open Book	69
CREAZIONE: *Canals in Venice*	73
Wood Palette	75
Chanting Gold Hymns	77
Walking with Beatniks	79
Minoan Islands	82
Day in Baltimore	84
About the Author	89
About the Artist	89
Acknowledgements	90

*"The dreamers of the day are dangerous people.
For they dream their dreams with open eyes,
and make them come true."*

~D.H. Lawrence

FOREWORD

ENDLESS is a book of diversity and inspiration, sensual, spiritual, exotic, and human; it is a work of profound and enduring beauty that represents the passionate and ephemeral, the mundane and the more-than-natural in precisely rendered artistry. This masterpiece is a gracious portrayal of the conceptual and material worlds as Anne Tammel ranges through the domains of literature, of earthly travel, of mortal experience and renewal, and in a truly Sapphic sense—of ultimate silence where the poet herself stands apart from both her work and the cosmos itself. These are the seven days of creation, and, as she herself remarks, the '*red silk journals are covered in sweat.*'

This poetry transforms the reader as it moves through the emotion and times of character, literature, and place—drawing our consciousness in its perfect wake; there is much profound learning in this book and its magisterial scales of language. To put the collection aside is suddenly to see the landscape in a new light where grey and white are perpetually moving but without invention or causality: for such is the mastery of the author that each phrase and metaphor, each image and *stanza*, resonates perfectly. As with all fine works, the combination and unison of the worldly with the impersonal-yet-subjective is immaculate; it is refreshing and rare to read such flawless poetry.

Tammel's use of implicit dialogue is a subtle technique which lifts the book toward another register, gently drawing the lyric into dramatic form. This is remarkable and uncommon, and is deftly accomplished, for the metonyms fuse and mortise without apparent seam. In fact, the book at large is a completely inclusive drama, such is the unity and accuracy of the sequence, and the work is as a *cycle*. One can imagine a performance of the collection, not as a book but a *duo* for voices—perhaps with accompaniment—for there is a clear sense of the operatic which supplies the poetry with a powerful yet delicate hypostatic coherence. This, apart from the poems themselves, offers the reader another dimension of pleasure and literary satisfaction: we are quite literally *in*-formed and delivered by the words.

'*Melodies glide on the air*' for Tammel as she gathers these experiences, and in her verbal refinement—where language becomes the substance of such life and being—the poems are effortless in detail, and yet without overt intentionality: such is singular mark of true genius in any genre or medium. '*The bronze cascading stones*' she witnesses in southern Greece are intrinsic to these aerial chimes; duality and the literary duplicity of sensation are the vehicle of so much of her world and the earthliness of human life, for Anne is able to remove herself from herself, much as Sappho would once do, and to engage simultaneously in so many lives and their physical topography, along with a concordant volatile shadowing. This is the significant weightlessness of her book, its terrific lucidity and its strongly forceful personification.

ENDLESS is a mantic book, the handiwork of a sorceress and *magicienne*, of one whose gifts with language and perception transform the sublunary and timely into pictures of dynamic affect: the indelible and the permanent, faultlessly charged with exact renditions of the mortal and sensible. In this process, the death of the universal feminine is translated into more than the simply temporal, as seasonality becomes unified into an idea that—like Socratic *form* and Platonic *harmony*—is indestructible and imperishable, for such is the true victory of this fully impressive and fabulous poetry with its myriad planes of *likeness*. My favourite image from the whole collection is that of the final ominous beauty, of '*euphoric wings*' and '*imaginary birds*,' as well-tempered metaphor and metonym weave the fabric of the song into an unbreakably refined *textus*; hence, *ENDLESS* is made into an object I return to frequently and continue to keep with me.

'*I was your breath—your sleepless instrument entwined with mine...we cried at the morning light, to tell the world...we lost as much in love as they...*'

Kevin McGrath, Harvard University

ENDLESS

A LITERATE PASSION

PASSIONE

That Red Red Sea

Amelia Earhart at the Red Sea

At the Red Sea
she is surprised
to discover the sea

not at all
red—
but blue.

Not remotely crimson
as she's allowed herself to imagine. Not
like the burning sun
she spent years
chasing—to capture.

> *All night I dreamt of the sea*
> *I dreamt of a place of wandering,*
> *of someone like you wanting*
> *a place like this*

"Why call it red if it's blue."
She sips palm wine with Fred
at Massawa, the last
stopping point
in Africa.

"Red mountains
near the shore—" he says,
the night air one-hundred-
and-six degrees, "seasonal
blooms give off an illusion
of red."

She gazes toward that blue Red
Sea, watches the hues of it
shift in the last late
day light.

"I was
expecting this all
to play out so
differently. I am
a different woman
here—there is a need
not to
go back."

>*And yet
>   all I dreamt of last night
>was the sea;
>   I tasted that sea on my lips
>   in dreams,
>I dreamt of tasting that
>   sea with you, your taste
>   intimate as that Red
>Red Sea—not even red
>   like you...
>but miles and
>   miles
>   of endless blue*

The sun dips. He turns
to Amelia: "That is
what you've wanted?"

>*I dreamt
>   last night
>   of someone
>like you, of
>   wanting you
>   wandering in
>   red—in
>   a place like this.*

The bright morning
following the blue of the Red
Sea, she needs to feel
it for herself. Dip her toes into
that water of mystery, know
for once…
the truth.

She reels
with the curiosity
of a child. And in
native grey
skirt, runs

toward that odd water's edge. Laughs
back at her own reflection in the rippling
rim of the northern-
most tropical sea, the sea
Herodotus in his leniency
toward fairy tales named
the *Southern Sea.*

She dances in that
early blush. Wonders
why she's waited
so long
to live…

Imagines herself
in a streaming hot bath,
swimming in circles
of bright
red
fish.

All night

I dreamt

of you,

of only you

in that

Red sea...

Lost inside that coral reef—
her quiet is broken in two

And yet

all night

I dreamt

of you

"Monsoons—" he calls

I dreamt

of the sea.

And I dreamt

of you–

In a way

    I became that sea—

        swimming with you.

She looks down to her dress
—a wet weighted garb
that now harnesses her.

She has been found in
her most private moment—
discovering who she
is becoming.

And yet

    I dreamt

        all night

            I drank that

                Sea, I drank

                  you in it;

I loved

        you and

    I loved

           you and me

                at that Red

                    Red Sea...

Paper Angels

Did you have wings?
Each limb reaching toward an open

sky, over New York. Spinning,
toppling. angelic, blackening

papers drift among you—
those snowflakes of September

scattered from open windows.
Could they have been the wings

of those who won't emerge,
releasing them to an expanse

we will not touch?
We will not know.

And will we ever
gather all of those papers?

You drift along-
side them, suspended,

momentarily—inhumanly
free, and only

for this split-second moment.
Will we ever know

what they were?
How many?

The question that fills each of
us as you topple through this odd

black morning: *Who
are you?* Why you choose

to lead this pattern
of papers that dances

into the sky-turned-
smoke—Icarian angels

rejecting despair, floating
high above us

on euphoric wings,
brave. Immortal,

lost…and

yet

somehow

momentarily

lofty.

Amelia and the Silken Sheet

There is
unsung possibility
in an airport tarmac
filled with morning sun—

a cognac color
fills the sky, blankets the
asphalt…surrounds
the mountains with the
muse of adventure.

> In the air, Fred peels the purple
> shell from a ripe sea almond,
> lifts the fruit
>
> to Amelia's lips. She tastes it as
> she muses at the ground that
> stretches its white arms below them.
>
> *Why rush back?* His
> eyes cross hers. Thunder-
> clouds roll behind them.
>
> *There is a danger, you know,*
> *in thinking that way…*She looks
> down. *In wanting to stay…*

In Karachi, the desert stretches
before them, an exotic unknown
invitation.

Heat rises from the earth—
awakens her senses in musical voices.
Travels her spine. She kneels.

It is a calling. He stares at
the weather, the raging sea, again
at Amelia. *For you to find that life…*

She bathes in hot desert wind, pulls odd-
scented water onto her cheeks. Looks
at the bold sun, stands with the sunset
and cognac tarmac behind her, says:

> *There is a place*
> *between the dark*
> *and the light*
> *where we often rest,*
> *knowing we don't need*
> *to choose sides:*
>
> *a silken sheet wrapped*
> *around our barest selves*
> *in the early light...*
>
> *For those who've*
> *heard the echo*
> *of our call,*
> *that silken sheet*
> *slips quickly away—the place*
> *of quiet quickly*
> *diminished—*
> *replaced*
>
> *by unrest, leaving*
> *us to face our own*
> *bare truths. Truths*
> *we don't always*
> *desire...*
>
> *It is up to us,*
> *what we decide*
> *to do*
>
> *with*
> *our*
> *truths.*

Blue Angels

The smell of stains
from tobacco fill their hands; they
sit playing cards by the sad
blue breeze on an old
folding card table
Thelen carried across
the planet. He says it
had been
on the Midway,

and I believe him.
My father looks
with bright blue eyes
to the ace in his hand. Bent
in low resignation, he taps
and hums, makes a music
with the cards. The cold
shot of brandy he sips
is caramel; he winces then
swallows, keeps
playing, laying down

the aces, keeps talking
of Brooklyn bridges, watching
swallowed light as it fades in the sky,
knowing that tomorrow they
will come right back
to play this all again.
To talk

of storms past Iwo Jima, blankets
over Iceland; of snowstorms
that threatened to swallow
them as they walked
from bar
to barracks;
barracks to bar.

In their quiet,
resignation, no one sees
them as they laugh
and roar, deal
cards, blow
smoke against
the Coronado wind
that crosses their stained,
forgotten hands; they

look with a knowing—
knowing no one actually can
see them anymore—they go back

to the aces, lay them down,
fold that table under the
moon to show

at 6am, to open
it all up
again…

Poland and the Thick Black Shoes

My father used to tap dance in thick black shoes,
dance all night on the winter kitchen floor, birds
elated in the blue night sky;

My father would tap dance on thick
kitchen floors; birds would rhyme. He
would sing his song, dance

'til dawn; birds would match those
altering sways. My father would dance
in those thick winter shoes, with speed,

swift rhyme, he would
tap dance all night; black
army shoes creating a song.

And when we woke, shivering and tired
eyed, ate rich ripe fruit—those dishes he'd
left, filled with Italian song;

all the cold night long, he would sing
blue time songs; dance memories away
as he cooked in the night—sang his songs.

In those thick World War
II shoes, he would dance to those
songs. To forget, he'd create

newer songs of New
York, and of Poland—he would sing
songs of snow; he would dance

on that thick kitchen floor. Matching
and rhyming, those black tiles would shine;
he would sway with the thick

army shoes in the black winter
night. He would sing when his thoughts turned
to Poland, to the blues; he would dance

to erase those blue time memories:
New York, a smoke-filled sky
—Poland, the night he sang,

New York, the night he sang. Poland,
a black-shoe memory, tap
in the dark winter night—from a song.

He would dance, he would
sing, he would dream, when he sang
about Poland—of New York

as he cooked, and he danced,
and he sang winter songs; he
would chase

winter blues
with those songs—when he sang
when he cooked, and he danced,
and he dreamt
all night long.

Imaginary Birds

In my dream
I went back
to my mother's house.

It was winter; she
sat at the edge
of my bed

while I slept—
shivering, as she would
early Saturdays

in my moonlit room, with
the Aurora Borealis-painted
plaster ceilings and moody skies.

This time, instead of
remembering my father, she
watched over me…

> *You only live once. You*
> *are what you dreamt you*
> *were. You are here.*

Lobster steamed
in the kitchen, a sky
of gray San Jose December;

Imaginary lavender vines
ran next to June birds outside—
the children of cool memories

in the city I love so much, with
the broken sidewalks, old-paned windows,
and the ghosts of all the shops that have now closed.

You only live once.
You are here—you are all
you dreamt you would be.

She could no longer
sleep. We both knew this—we
both remembered the November night

she could not talk to me; the dawn
slowly coming and the birds
outside circling nervously.

That night, she looked at me:
Don't tell me. I said. *I
know.* She looked again.

She knew, all
I needed
was to sleep

at my mother's house,
to dream by her side,
to dream

about birds, to count
pantomimes,
to write.

MAGIA

Fire, Sage and Mist

She Dreamt

she'd been a sorceress, healing witch
        gathering branches alone in dark woods.
Fusing herbs, she'd dwelt like this
        leaving suburbia in shadowed clouds.

Muds, flowers, poultices filled her small home,
        herbs steamed from tiny pots, bottles lined shelves
Odd tinctures healed strangers—even herself:
        black willow. arnica. cardamom. spice.

She ran toward the moon as they turned out their lights,
        sought earth and its pattern, night after night—
sang with moonlight, fire, sage, and mist,
        carried gifts from the old, summoned the wise.

At dawn, when they woke to yawn about dreams,
she turned to her books, to the night—to new schemes.

Fire, Spice and Zen

fire, spice & I,
we live in unison.
our tempered forces meet

in a small kitchen; in bare feet
at my burner, they think
i am the pitiful. no, *the power*.

i laugh, and think of
cinnamon, absinthe, rows
and rows of bottles prepared

by small women. we meet at
morning's light to discuss the
zen and yin of them.

at night, when apricot-azure flames
come ripping in, filtered
by wild winds, night circling

and howling in, i am preparing
a sorceress' cycle, a sin. those scents
that began in intuition

meet evening.
and in health, chi,
culinary sin,

I offer my circling,
healing soup to you,
master, and you begin

to feel you
are ruler, and I,
a servant?
think again.

Ominous Structures

A man once
warned me of Mephistopheles,
Incorporated: *I'm arming you
with magic dust.* He chanted
tropes...metonymy,
anaphora,
synecdoche.

*Remember the power
you carry,* he said, *when
they try to own you...know the
possibility of your influence.
Walk away.*

Months later, I ran into
those shining buildings—caught
in the mirrors, the panache, the name, forgot
who I was. Gave sleepless nights, my words
and plans—dreams bought
then sold by circling sharks
and minions, spinning, chiseling
at the truth each night
to emerge more
powerful, polished
at dawn.

One night, late, I watched
my reflection in a window
over the sea
of cars on the 101:

> *My words spun
> magic dust...and
> ominous plans turned
> profits*

*for all who used them—
increased their
desire.*

I lay my head
on silken sheets
under a Palo
Alto moon and stars…

*Still myself, in a dream, but fifteen
again at a seaside café, I sketched
fragments of poems on hand-
woven notes, shoved drafts
aside. A frantic foreign
man mechanically set
a large bill
on one.*

*I asked
why. He would
only point—shake his
head with fearful eyes
toward the ominous geometric
structure, so large it
darkened the July sky,
cast shadows
where July
sun should
have been.*

At morning, with
open eyes and empty
hands, I left…

a poet.

Candlelight
The Lonely Pond

Away from the world...earth and ocean essences
travel in water, rhyme with candlelight: *ylang
ylang, cedar, sandalwood, thyme.* Oils infuse,
create new light—new atmosphere in my echoing
bath on this windy night..

A white lotus flower is my core.

I break the seal of this heavenly
bottle; watch the world
spill in. Night
rings in euphonious
songs. I step in
to glowing water ...

Deep, central source of illumination.

I awaken in herbs, new flowers—

*So rich, very rich, this enlightening
secret, echoing...awakening...
impenetrable...true. This force,
this emanating strength carries elixirs
through my veins...exudes health,
peace, deep spiritual heat, rhythm,
trust, rejuvenating
harmony ...*

In tune with night's sounds—a new
candlelit spirit-filled song...this
state of meditativeness...of
magnificence...breathes
me in...

Selene
Moonrise Over Oia

She glows, tangerine behind the blunt
powdered cliffs that line Akrotiri, the
ancient city only half unearthed. Does
anyone know her secret? *She sings;*

her mystical notes cross all of Oia,
that Greek island north of Crete. Above
white cliffs, sun burns to twilight. Sky
fills with dusk. All turn to watch her rise, burn red

above the Aegean—summon the night.
Tall women dance beneath her. Each
sends forth her own ancient symbols—prayers
for the night—for the mystical light

that circles the sky. Selene looks back to
search the illumined earth—*to find Endymion.*

VITA DELL'ALDILÀ

Euphoric Wings

Proliferative Ashes
For Paul Celan

You shiver on roofs.
When it is cold, I watch slivers of
icicles drip slowly. Then stopping,
you sing to us. Even after

you swam into that river,
I hear your voice, I see the eyes
of those you remember, singing
behind the dismissive shock,
the cold black grates.

I think of typhus,
little broken cups,
insolent worms,
iced fingertips,
black-caked with dust
of early age. The days
all black
with soot and hell.

And you
poet-dreamer
rising in the sky

above proliferative ashes,
singing, dying
so very many times…

I dreamt I met
with you
in those clouds,
brought perennial herbs, smooth
blankets, white milk, clean skin,
a bath, some French,
and undisturbed German.

We turned back
the language, you
and I, like chimes
on a clock.

We hid up there
in the sky, turned
those numbers back
so there could be none

left—I created new
languages with you—we
sang unmentionable
words, as if

we could
ever touch
those
dreams.

Streets of Florence

The dust of lonely souls lines these streets.
In breath-like tempos, we hear its chiming
songs: *A–Cru–ce Sa–lut*…At the Duomo, we
crouch on old wood in the hot sun and pray
where Dante wept, and where the gilded doors
delivered small, frail souls to paradise.
Today, the sweetshop sells espresso shots
above those dust-lined tombs. Layers upon
layers of streets, and cities—this site, this
city were built for pagan gods, we learn,
as we gaze toward that dome in bewildered
wonder, wonder if the damned could fly.
You and I walk out toward dusk, the dome,
a museum. Souls reach the air with song…

Double Sunrise
Anne Morrow to Charles Lindbergh

I think of you
in the sky, wings
vast, ever-present.

I, lonely moon
shell on land, humming
for your advancement. Knowing
nothing of other wives. Only words
carved into island sands

singing, advancing: *come
down, come meet
on level ground.*

I thought I would fly
toward you with wings soft
and lonely, struggle to touch
the safety of your clouds—
the singularity of your flight.
Seek the sameness of breath

in the *fragile perfection*
of our double sunrise—
soft opaque shell that housed two
flawless halves, bound with only
one hinge, meeting
one another at
every point…

now nothing but a *forgotten*
mystery, our secret, empty
world
unto
itself…

Tohoku
March 11, 2011

The day the earth
moved
eight feet,
I wanted to slip
my hands
into those
waters,

shout:
no, breathe!

I wanted to pull
you out
among the kelp,
the lost and missing
souls—forgotten whales
and bones—

I wanted to
resuscitate you,
make you swim, reel
you back in, a tiny minnow
reaching toward the broken
shore, a life—

summed up
in a haplessly
swimming tail.

I pictured myself
painting your broken buildings,
placing each of them carefully back
into that intricate set of
structures built
on that ring
of fire.

I wanted to run
to those dark
grey waters,
dig deep
beneath
their surface, through
the mystery and
muck and the
sands of
salvation,

pull the entire earth
back onto
its axis;

I wanted
you to
breathe.

PERDITA

In the Silent Light

Kerouac in San Francisco

The water runs still, like friends who mix patinas,
play stringed instruments and write books, yet say little.
The buildings shine water. Those one-way streets
that line the buildings are mazes; they make no sense.

We walk to the Embarcadero, see the oldest light
house at Alcatraz, wonder at the souls who swam
from it at night, realize you yourself are one of those souls
looking for something, always searching—yet finding nothing.

> *Kerouac walked there once*
> *with empty pockets;*
> *passed Italian cafes,*
> *spoke words, like jazz,*
>
> *looked only in windows—*
> *sat in empty kitchens,*
> *wrote bourgeois tragedy*
> *through dharma hunger.*

We walked all night one December, past mid-
night to reach that bridge; it was there I saw you
had no promises to keep for me, San Francisco…
You were filled with only desire, and chill

—the bitter, sweet aftertaste of a lonely
night with distant friends, disenchanted wanderers
who walk searching for something, some mystical light
they came to discover they'd never find.

> *He spent his evening once*
> *staring out at water, smoking and*
> *wishing he were not alone. And yet*
> *it was only while alone that he could think.*

When we drove away from that
water, there were only mists—gray and
distant memories, smoke that dissipates—
those watercolor, stringed instrument songs—of you.

> *He woke before everyone, played*
> *forgotten jazz records, then limped*
> *to the all-night liquor store, where he bought*
> *just enough hope to fill a paper bag.*

Unripe Peaches

and though we stumbled across the other,
we listened, like blue light dawn, asking
why we must survive, like fruit, to gently ripen,
burst open, then pare down on drooping
stems at the close of dusk.

how does a peach grow when plucked from its source,
and fall to ripen in silent remorse?

when we asked where he was going, he gave us
a bank account and a life, never
an answer.   those branches swayed
mightily toward the east, the dream,
we struggled to believe. so
we waited for his vast return, battered
suitcases flapping in wind, night falling in. we pictured
him racing toward us, to avoid the night engulfing him
one more time—

and while we waited in our overflowing
garden as fruit trees, flowers, and rainwater
dripped into our dreams, we searched for
one tree that could satiate real needs; and made
up a life, savoring unripe fruit, picking
rich rose petals from stems. *he loves me.*
sometimes even eating them. *loves me not.*

and what a father: giver of gifts, man in crisp
black jackets, wandering new york city
streets at night, searching
for some kind of life.

how does a peach grow when plucked from its source
and late-night wind blows in silent remorse?

our dreams were chased by the etches of
a thinning night.   at dawn, when we woke with
tired eyes and dusky plans, realizing he
was still not home, ate rich pate and fruit we'd
left for him. in the silent light,
we came to know a man who'd never come
to know this home.

months later, phones would ring from echoing
train stations. could he get a ride?
mom, cooking dinner, too busy to drive. the cab
would shuttle in a frozen man, tired, clothes
too bold, too crisp, too formal for california.

he would talk of the mother in new york he
wished we knew, and we would believe, sharing
unripe peaches, picked early from branches, listening,
with bright, unripe
eyes of childhood.

Marilyn

The curtains hung limp
the day they rolled
her away. She smiled
through that bright
August morning

with hypnotic eyes
closed, and the blue
red lips from a forgotten
glossed pinup…she knew
to the world, she

was Marilyn, that
va-va elusive movie
star wrapped in nothing
but a white dime-store
sheet, who made men
burn with the sweat and
mystery and empty
shimmer of that silver
screen. She waited
'til the cars,

the buses, the limousines
and carriages, the hearse
had all gone home—'til
that LA sun turned
broad and faded—
then she wept.

> My mother walked alone at dawn,
> the day they discovered her father
> on his church steps. She walked
>
> the sunrise streets of New York
> in a smart black dress,
> 1951 pearls and

no shoes at dawn;
then all the way
back home, making her
way down Fifth:
always punctual, so
punctuated in shiny black
coats, impeccably dressed. She
didn't know
how to stop
for death.

So she stayed up all
that gloomy-day night
watching Brooklyn fade
from her open window, eating
stale crackers, scraping dimes
together to buy Italian
wine at the corner. In
the morning, she
walked back through the dawn-
lit streets of Manhattan alone.

Marilyn ran at night, at dawn. She ran
through pain as the trucks rolled past
her Beverly Hills roads, to
make it home, and hide in
newer sets of pearls from
the homes of men
who took everything—
who sent her
out to
the cold
with a row of pills, of
pictures, and a bottle of
Dom—the bottle
she tucked in-
to the borrowed
mink coat.

My mother ran
enterprises, fled Love
Canal floods and wounded
hearts, to lead two every snow-
drenched day through
night…into
dawn.

Marilyn led
a persona: refined,
impeccable—the dream, the stars
at night, the moon and panache
we all thought we wanted…and yet
it was a flighty star-
dom, her fleeting
aquiline image—a gilded, white-

sheet wrapped McCarthy-
era façade. Lost woman
afraid of a kitchen, burnt
by an aftertaste of too many
men; she could not speak for
herself, so she wrote it, and
ran from their houses—

a brilliant woman,
who could only
ever actualize
a series
of pictures, of
iridescent
smiles, and
broken
hearts—who
could not
stop to
live…

SPIRITO

Mystical Minoan Chimes

Dante and the Silk Journal

One morning, in Florence, I walked with Dante
Alighieri. We strolled mile after mile of dusty city
streets, past dawn till

we reached the Arno, where Dante, in his hand-
crafted flat leather shoes and red velvet cloak, offered
a rich purple Florentine plum. *Neutrality*

does not suit you. He looked into me then
through me with eyes of foreboding: *Who
are you?* Leaves fluttered. Dante took my

red journal from my hands. *Look past
your mortal life.* I dropped the too-
ripe plum. Leaves shifted

to shades of autumn as wind
rushed past us. *Everyone is allowed
to go mad...once per year.* Dante

handed me his own worn journal, filled with
words, with drawings of purple plums and
private scarlet notes. He nodded as he walked

through that colorful Florentine crowd
toward the Duomo, my own secret journal
tucked under his arm. I tried with unsteady legs

to rush after the poet, through the clang and the clamor
of those ancient city streets, along that uneven
cobblestone road, only to discover—

I

was

falling…

Gates of Paradise
Polythene Wings

I walk a lonely Italian winding road. It is late summer. Sun
falls; colors drift on wind. Night air dries. Around me,
plums fall from branches, grapes ripen on vines.

I used to dream of downtown, living in San Jose—find
Anaïs Nin books, sit and write, dream of days like this.
And yet on days like this I dream of why I woke wishing
for a darkening street in Italy, robed in sun, creating songs in
the rough Florentine earth.

Bodies upon bodies ascended there, angels waiting to slip
through those Gates of Paradise—lovers who lost and loved,
lived, ate, and wept at those gates, hoping to catch one glimpse
of heaven, listening for chimes. Waiting, singing at
those gates, writing at those gates…

I fill my house with amber lights: wait for the polythene feel—
wings of angels behind me. Fill my head with flights each day,
a trip to Florentine heaven, like the scribes who pored hour after
hour over handcrafted paper, bled ink from *pomegranates,
thistle milk, indigoes, cloves*, lit by paling tallow candles.

Men have sung on those steps. I have dreamt on them—
that lonely sun illuminating the burning eternal progress
in the distance. In some ways, Florence speaks like
no other city—Florence will always call—invoke
the sounds of the spirit, and welcome those who
wait, wide-eyed at those gates, for
one glimpse of
an angel on
new polythene
wings, one lonely
soul preparing to make
its solitary
passage…

Athênai

On the shuttle from the airport,
the scalding terrain reminds us
we are far from America. We pass unfinished
structures, surrounded by miles and stretching

miles of nothing but sun that beats into and
through them. They rise from the rough dry
earth—abandoned ruins or forgotten crosses.
And people here are exquisite paintings,

with deep dark eyes and expressive lips—their
voices, a music we will never truly understand
but long to hear again, again, and yet even
again at dawn. Fading vehicles carry us to worlds

forgotten, with ancient treasures that bear signs of the
new just above the old. In Athens, the broken stone
roads toward Acropoli hum with motorized scooters.
They kick up the dust of unnamed souls far

beneath these roads. The language of locals and motors
form a static song that hums throughout the night, and into
days, and into more and more of these arid, stretching nights.
And still we walk these dusty, narrow roads of late after-

noon, sip Fanta from small bottles, wait
for the myths to envelope us even in our dreams,
fold us into this forgotten world, transform us
into people with exotic

eyes and intangible charms—those voices
the world longs to hear again, again, and yet
even again in the first, faintest musical
sounds
of
dawn...

Leaving Paris
Zelda to F. Scott Fitzgerald

In this lonely-fated ship,
I sail in velvet dress, veiled
in black cape and hat. Alone,

I seek freedom from the madness—
from you. The waters they promised
are not blue—not purple. Beyond

the Atlantic, my only comfort,
a café in Greenwich, above which
you and I once slept. Bodies

breathed in steamy street
air. Diaries filled with
words of you…of you

and the flamboyant art
you would take
away but could not give.

The sage-femme says, *now
tout d·accord*; the only swell,
the empty bits of leftover heart

she did not take, she could
not take. I walk the rainy streets
in painted hats, drink rich

plum wine, and dance
with men I never met. The life
I will not, cannot forget,

that life I
gave away
so you
could
write…

AURORA BOREALE

Milkweed Honey, Pure Saffron Desire

Paradiso
Eros & Psyche

we swept in summer nights, lie still
when love was sublime and reachable

as the pale green sky above that ocean's rim.
when you engaged in song

i was your breath—your sleepless instrument entwined
with mine. exhaling was like singing; rang in tune

with dew on our lips and your sinewy desire
enveloping mine, invented for your touch.

like flower petals, we cried at morning light
breaking through to day, to tell the world

—we lost as much in love—
as they, in death.

Endless
Anaïs Nin to Henry Miller

My search for you is endless…
Searching, seeming
like a wife, an insatiable wife…a lover
of silk, and words, and your breath.

You taunt me; a lost child rests
at the tip of my torture. Your torment
travels through me as I travel
morning trains, and cafes—

Paris, and ships to Spain—and then
America…where I will fight
not to remember
your name.

An endless list of lovers, knowing only
my totality, my *silhouette parfaite*. If they knew—
if they were seized by you—seized
by your words, fighting to forget
the *supreme immolation*
of the ego: motherhood,
that endless,
volatile curse…

And Hugh waits, an endless trail
of dull husbandry; I wait
an endless amount of time,
until our lives
have become dust
and history,

and red silk journals
are covered
in sweat
and
secrets…

Dinner Couplets

Silver rosemary stalks and
elliptical leaves

of thyme
glow with candlelight

and Saint-Estephe we choose
before midnight around the corner

as moon pours on our backs,
and we pick pungent jasmine

stems then crush
them to release the scent—

At home, we dress
small gold plates

in flowers and herbs,
watch moon filter through

that moody window, shine fragile
glasses you pour cloudy cabernet

into—triple-crème *Délice* should
be infused with lavender,

served only with jazz, or songs that
sound like home—

I search for spice, chanterelles,
Amontillado; impatient

cupboards throw unwanted bottles
out. Our small table overflows

with projects and stories
I clear away for the tray

of moon and desire—
We used to dine

on imagination,
truffles, and wine,

inviting people to dance
at Moody Road, the trees outside

inviting them back—for evenings
and evenings of wonder…

Now we pass
through this small place,

burn candles, search for a real
home as we pretend

each time I cook, we are in
love with this little place, and eat.

Autumn, Love, and Pomegranate Pears

At early dusk,
we gather...

harvest wine
the juice of one pomegranate
a half cup of coconut sugar
grated tangerine peel
one cinnamon stick,
and two ripe Bosc pears

The sky dims;
I light a new candle...

In a small
saucepan, I stir Syrah-
Port, pomegranate juice
and coconut sugar
with the cinnamon
stick and tangerine
peel then wait
for the sugar
to dissolve.

We sip port from small
glasses, watch the sky

I peel and core
both pears from
the bottom wide
ends, trim them
flat then stand
upright in
a small porcelain
dish, pour the
Port-Pomegranate
sauce over,
and roast

at 375 for
one hour;

*He opens the window; cool rushes
in. We stare at the moon...*

I pull the dish
from the oven, pour
the juices into a sauce
pan then simmer on
the stove to
create a
glaze.

*He picks up his saxophone,
plays some jazz...*

On small filigreed
plates, I arrange
the pears and
pour the Port
Pomegranate
glaze over each.

*He lights a fire;
it fills the room with amber...*

I serve the autumn
pears warm
with vanilla
gelato.

*We fall in love
all over again...
with Autumn....*

Moon an Open Book

The world is
not ambitious
tonight.

The moon hangs
low. I live in the sky—
its dark side

reflecting silent curves,
in subtle unison
with pure intention.

That moon
is a book; I savor
forbidden pages—

a crisp pear, fleur
de sel beurre, truffle,
pate, indigo herbs—

words spread across it;
the pages can cut
if turned too quickly—

out of breath in these
quiet moments, reflecting
desires, touched by that moon,

which cares nothing for
ambition…only the rich
pause for breath, new words:

milkweed honey,
newly ripened figs–pure
saffron desire…

CREAZIONE

Canals in Venice

Wood Palette

On the deck, overlooking
white Coronado waves,
he washes yellow mountains
into teal light skies, then whispers
as walls are built. She stands
in vineyards. He takes away the vines
and they resurface, crimson; then
begins his daily trip, slave to the inner
rhythm, where

>*Blue*
>Swarms in rich apples,
>walks in the puddles
>and gathers crisp ripples
>like

>*Green*
>Rhymes with silent sounds of purple
>meadows, wet capes and the lap
>of quiet lotus petals
>swimming in

>*White*
>Enfolding yellow stamens of
>marigolds, releasing ancient oils,
>and eliciting lifelike sounds
>like

>*Russet*
>Rich hills where native sweat
>lodges wait for women, seasons
>churn and the undulating wheel of life
>still burns.

He soaks his brush in silk-shallow water
stares at the sun in shifts, stands back
to glide through slight canals in Venice,
sip afternoon wine with a dark-haired goddess—
mixes metal with yellow, sand with seeping
wind, and sings patiently, *this wood palette feels like sin*
then turns in the easel, puts on his hat
and hopes to sell two cars again.

Chanting Gold Hymns

It was the New Millennium;
we were young in it.
New lights twinkled
from seaside houses; boats
sailed with *instant-aires* who knew nothing
but that they wanted to chase some half-
planned dream of sailing seas like conquerors
who ruled everything.

"Intellectual Property" took on a new meaning.
Starbucks lights shone from every metropolitan
intersection, a beacon on rainy days. A new
Christianity was on the rise; mega-evangelists
stood at their pulpits inviting millions to step on
up and be instantly saved, all for reading their
bestselling book then saying you believe. Everything
was attainable. CEOs napped under Palo Alto
desks then drove jalopies through mists of
dawn for two hours sleep. They would head back to
earn another million from an engine they'd
built exclusively for the cyber realm.

We were the last of the dreamers—still
laughed Saturday mornings, floating candles
on smooth lotus petals in the bath, chanting
yogi hymns, believing they would somehow
transform us. We believed in
and sought out the impossible.

He kept looking forward; I continued
to look back, to repair the broken past; my
parents had travelled back east to the furthest
west, where they could still reach
land and chase the dream. Catch
the golden ring.

Surrounded by invention,
pioneering spirit, determination
to turn the impossible into a new
reality. And to do so under
stars as the rest of the world slept.

In this juxtaposition of time, space and
two unique lives, we were opposites, intertwined
from the start, growing up miles apart…me
roller skating endlessly down a dandelion-
lined street in San Jose sun, picking new
apricots from branches, reciting lines of old poets
mixed with seventies lyrics, heading to Santa
Cruz on sunny days for herbs in hemp-lined shops…
he running through juniper covered hills, books
of equations in his pockets, creating a private
communications network through his phone…

All while the Wonderful Wizard of Woz
worked miles away in his garage, twining small
wires together, focusing into late night
hours, breathing in summer flowers
as night rolled into day and he hummed in
the hot morning sun…to change the world
with his someday plan…

We were the dreamers who came
from opposite shores, bound together in
the steamy moment my poetics mixed
with his genius…catching that gold
in myths, rhyming with white
lotus; skating and dreaming,
inventing,
believing…

Walking with Beatniks

Walking late
one autumn San
Jose afternoon,

we cross Market
in long black coats, shield
our faces from wind.

Bobbie speaks of Neal
Cassady, showing up for dinner—Jack's
hatred for women, his letter
during her third pregnancy:

Did she '*really want to
introduce another gentle soul
into this vile, cursed place?*'

She shivers, talks of Creeley
resenting her writing—Anne
remembering him screaming, banging
on locked doors of the study
as the women hid to chant songs
and words…poetic verse.

Bobbie says he
dropped acid as *a
way to overcome
alcoholism—stop
the war—a
power* in the sixties
*to change
everyone, our
thoughts, relationships, our
everything.*

Anne adds, Yes—with
chanting passion, *you
feel the electricity
of everything
happening. One trip
with Allen, a wild
wet mushroom was taking
over the world—a massive
bomb encompassing
everything. At
the end of the night,
it was my
BandAid.*

The sage slips
into the Fairmont,
sleepy-eyed, silk
violet dress flowing
behind—with autumn leaves.

Bobbie stops
to question
Carolyn's innocence—still
Carolyn's blind innocence—always
managing to endure
such vile men:

*I can't help but know
men in heterosexual groups
fuck one woman*

*and relate to one another
as homosexuals. It
happens all the time...*

then graciously turns to leave, long
black coat toward
that autumn evening, sky
quickly darkening,
hair, like scattered
leaves, lost,
paradisiacal,
flowing…

Minoan Islands

Its rocks jut out to sea;
forgotten blend of
land, dark salt, and
the bones
of those forgotten
washed
ashore—

their egos like
minions
that rush to rocks
then recede. Short lived, vibrant, so transitory.

I wonder
on this small jut of an island, its rocky bit of land
that reaches out to an endless sea,
why I was called. This end
of the world—

of a place, where one
could so easily be dismissed, their own
life a minion or minnow, sad
swimming fish with
one tail, lost sight
of its pack;

the tourists swim in Speedos. They
hike with backpacks, wonder
as they pass at
the fateful symmetry of tortured isles:
they search for wood, dark currants, lost
ore. They ask: *Will the gods awaken–spit*
stones like Talos, cast
bronze, and fire
in all directions?

Those tourists march further up that hill, swim
in sun, sunbathe on flat rocks, board
boats to island shacks, share beer, fresh
fish reeled wildly from those seas on rusted
wires; the beer, the fish, the seas—it is all
transparent, those swimming waters
that buried millions. The tourists laugh;

they swim back home, hear mystical Minoan
chimes at night; think volcanic ash. They taste
it on their lips in dreams. They dream at times
of being fish—those scattered minnows washed ashore—
their scintillating fins splash ruefully as water turns.

I sit as sun rushes down, wonder
as water rushes toward my ankles:
Why was I called?
Asking only for air, amassed in layers
of clouded memories, I ask again, *why*
must I return to watch
those bronze
cascading
stones…

Day in Baltimore

The day they warned
of freezing rain, I drove
that heavy rented sedan

toward St. Joseph's.
Blue air was thick.
Massive trees swayed.

The Charles Street
homes called me toward
their darkening charm;

some released patients
to that lonely hospital, where
I would sit, in aqua scrubs,

tight mask gagging but could
not, for anything, keep out
the wandering smell of blood.

Room four was bitter, silent,
cold. In rolled the stiffened
woman. From a window, high

by a clock on the wall,
we could see the rain start
in dense dark sheets—to fall

then freeze to bitter snowflakes.
The woman made no sound as
a tight-lipped man shouted

in her ears then dressed her
in gaudy tubes to have her
chest plate removed. She stared

past all of us, somehow watching
sun through that snow-rain. We knew
as they prepped her with trembling

hands what would swim
in whispers later: the surgeon
could not do valves.

Room three had no window
—just a tired perfusionist who
laughed his way through

our twelve-hour day, boasted
of an iron bladder, pumped
life back into the morning

man, who'd been reopened. I shivered,
pictured rain falling into snowflakes,
and wondered about the woman. Watched

the man, still and solemn, pull
us into his timely world, making me
forget New York, the night before.

The angry surgeon, surrounded
by wise women, whispered 'til breath-
like sounds filled one corner

then another—each heart
resuscitating with blood
before they swam back

toward the man, sewn
to life.   Midnight plane
to Boston. Hundreds of lights

soundlessly beating—those
saddened, short breaths.
The snowflakes

falling in

each

of

us.

About the Author

Author of the collection *Paper Angels* (Aldrich Press), Anne Tammel's works of fiction and poetry have appeared in journals and anthologies throughout America and Europe, most recently in *Poydras Review, Mediterranean Poetry, 3Elements Literary Review, Philadelphia Review of Books, Edgar Allan Poet Literary Journal, Annapurna Magazine, Clarify Culinary Anthology, Heaven and Hell Anthology, Sisters Born, Sisters Found: A Diversity of Voices, Life and Legends,* and many others. A Silicon Valley native, brand strategist, and literary figure who has brought poetic awareness to San Clemente, Tammel is founding owner of Poets and Dreamers, the literary organization and fine arts journal featured in CBS Los Angeles. Tammel is also owner of the executive branding and admissions firm, Tammel Enterprises. More about Anne and her works can be found at www.annetammel.com.

About the Artist

Eric Anfinson is an artist living and working in Key West, Florida. Anfinson, a native of Minnesota, paints full time from his Mockingbird Studio. A self trained painter, his work appears in collections throughout the North America and Europe. "*Art is everything and sometimes simply an essence. It is the tool that I use and that uses me in return. It is my best and most critical friend. But these words mean nothing by themselves, the work, the active process, is what matters most.*" To view more of Anfinson's work visit ericanfinson.com.

Acknowledgements

I extend my gratitude to the editors of the following journals and anthologies in which poems from *Endless: A Literate Passion* first appeared, sometimes in a slightly different form.

Poydras Review: "Wood Palette"

Edgar Allan Poet Literary Journal II: "Double Sunrise: Anne Morrow to Charles Lindbergh"

Edgar Allan Poet Literary Journal II: "When She Woke"

Saint Julian Press: "Amelia Earhart at the Red Sea"

Saint Julian Press: "Tohoku, March 11, 2011"

Mediterranean Poetry: "Selene: Moon Rise Over Oia"

Mediterranean Poetry: "Dante and the Red Silk Journal"

Mediterranean Poetry: "Athênai"

Miracle Literary Magazine: "Minoan Islands"

Annapurna Magazine: "Secrets of the Immortals"

Clarify Anthology 2014: "Dinner Couplets"

Clarify Anthology 2015: "Autumn, Love, and Pomegranate Pears"

Life and Legends: "Leaving Paris: Zelda to F. Scott Fitzgerald"

Life and Legends: "Unripe Peaches"

Life and Legends: "Amelia and the Silken Sheet"

Life and Legends: "Kerouac in San Francisco"

Heaven and Hell, Scream Magazine: "Proliferative Ashes: *For Paul Celan*"

Interstices: "Streets of August"

Paper Angels: "Paper Angels"

Paper Angels: "Day in Baltimore"

Paper Angels: "Imaginary Birds"

This book could not have happened without the many generous spirits who shared their poetic genius, unique artistic wisdom and uncommon support along the way. I am so honored to have collaborated with artist Eric Anfinson, who painted the exquisite work *"Anais and Henry"* after reading my book. I thank poets Marian Haddad, Lois P. Jones, and Mick Spillane for their wise and generous manuscript insights. I so appreciate my publisher, Ron Starbuck, for his commitment to artistic vision. And Craig Tammel, my husband, for believing in all my dreams and making them come true with me. Each has devoted countless hours to craft this work into a meaningful gift I now share with the world.

Illustrations:
Duomo in Tuscany, pg. 1: Mike Demidov/Shutterstock
Medical Herbs Medical Herbs and Plants, pg. 21: Geraria/Shutterstock
Little Swallows, pg. 31: ARaspopova/Shutterstock
Apricot Tree by Jules Trousset-1891 Paris, pg. 41; Lynea/Shutterstock
Decorative Grapes, pg. 53: Olga Mishyna/Shutterstock
Wine, Vineyard, Tuscany, pg. 63: Canicula/Shutterstock
Venice-Fondamenta Rio Marin, pg. 73: Viktoriya/Shutterstock